A New Frontier

The Peace Corps
in Eastern Europe

Brent Ashabranner

Photographs by Paul Conklin

COBBLEHILL BOOKS/Dutton
New York

Library of Congress Cataloging-in-Publication Data
Ashabranner, Brent K., date.
A new frontier : the Peace Corps in Eastern Europe / Brent
Ashabranner ; photographs by Paul Conklin.
p.   cm.
Includes index.
ISBN 0-525-65155-1
1. Peace Corps (U.S.)—Europe, Eastern—Juvenile literature.   2. Europe,
Eastern—Economic conditions—1989—Juvenile literature.   3. Europe,
Eastern—Social life and customs—Juvenile literature.   [1. Peace Corps
(U.S.)—Europe, Eastern.   2. Europe, Eastern—Social life and customs
3. Europe, Eastern—Economic conditions.]
I. Conklin, Paul, ill.   II. Title.
HC60.5.A843   1994   361.6—dc20   93-38535   CIP   AC

Published in the United States by Cobblehill Books,
an affiliate of Dutton Children's Books,
a division of Penguin Books USA Inc.,
375 Hudson Street, New York, New York 10014
Designed by Joy Taylor
Printed in the United States of America
First Edition   10 9 8 7 6 5 4 3 2 1

In memory of
STEPHEN FRANKLIN GREEN
who learned about the Peace Corps
when he was young.

Contents

1

"What You Can Do For Your Country"

Mealtime at the shelter. One of the boys pulls at Tom Ritter to get his attention.

THE SHELTER for homeless children in the Romanian capital of Bucharest is a small building separated from the busy street by a courtyard and a seven-foot wall. The shelter's capacity is forty-five children, and those lucky enough to be admitted—the doors open at seven o'clock in the evening—will receive a hot meal and a bed for the night. Thousands of homeless children roam the streets of Bucharest, but there is only one other shelter in the city.

As seven o'clock approaches, the children come like an invading army, desperate to be among the fortunate few. They try to force their way through the gate. They scale the wall. They jump from the wall to the shelter roof, dropping into the courtyard. The shrill cries of the children swell to an ear-piercing din. If you have heard that sound, you will never forget it. If you have seen that sight, you will remember it forever.

Tom Ritter sees these children in ragged clothes and hears their cries every night. Tom is a Peace Corps volunteer member of the small shelter staff. He is twenty-eight and has been toughened by work in soup kitchens and a shelter for homeless men in Chicago before joining the Peace Corps. But nothing can toughen you enough for the sight of these children, frantic for a plate of food and a warm, safe bed. Tom tries to keep order as they enter the shelter on a first come, first admitted basis, but he watches for girls and very young children and gives them preference.

When the last street child is admitted, Tom helps get them settled enough to start the meal. The tiny dining room holds only two tables, each of which seats eight, so the feeding goes on through three rotations. Two of the youngest boys, no more than six or seven years old, are as starved for affection and attention as they are for food. They cling to Tom while he works.

Tom sometimes stays at the shelter for a twenty-four-hour shift. When he stays all night, he fortifies himself with many cups of coffee and does not sleep. In that way he can make sure that bigger boys do not bully smaller ones and that there is no stealing. The children will get a good night's rest even if he doesn't.

JANICE HEMPHILL is having a Peace Corps experience very different from Tom Ritter's. She is a teacher in Kurdzhali, Bulgaria, a small city not far from Bulgaria's border with Greece and Turkey. Janice teaches English in a high school that emphasizes language learning. When Paul Conklin went to her school to take photographs, Janice asked him to talk to one of her classes so that they could hear a native English speaker besides herself. Paul told the students about his work as a photographer and then asked if they had any questions.

"Where do you live?" a girl wanted to know.

"I live in the capital of the United States," Paul said. "Do you know where that is?"

"Washington, D.C.," the girl replied.

"What famous person lives in Washington, D.C.?" Paul asked.

Janice Hemphill.

A boy put up his hand. "The President of the United States," he said.

"Where does the president live in Washington?" Paul asked.

Another boy held up his hand and said, "The White House."

"Why is it called the White House?" Paul asked.

That question seemed to stump the class at first, but then the girl who asked the first question spoke again. "I think it is called the White House," she said, "because it is white."

Janice is proud of her students. "They're very sharp," she told Paul. "They are just completing their first month of English study."

Janice Hemphill is from Denver and has a master's degree in teaching English as a foreign language from the University of Colorado. For years she taught English to immigrants in Denver and also taught in public schools. Janice is one of an increasing number of older Americans who are now joining the Peace Corps. She is sixty-five and bursting with energy that she pours into her work. In addition to full-time teaching at the high school, she teaches an adult English class in her apartment two nights a week.

"I sometimes think everyone in Bulgaria wants to learn English," she says.

A great desire to learn about America has bloomed since the toppling of the Communist government in Bulgaria in 1989. Soon after she arrived in Kurdzhali, Janice was asked to put on a two-week seminar for the Bulgarian Friends of America Society that was formed after the revolution. Her seminar sessions covered such topics as the U.S. Constitution, our election process, and the structure of our government at the national, state, and local levels. She used videos and slides friends from home had sent showing how average Americans live. Over fifty people came to the seminar; even the mayor of Kurdzhali attended.

"I've been fortunate," Janice says. "People are so generous and caring here. They check on me all the time, bring me things to eat. I have many friends at my school; but I have enlarged my circle, and now I have artist friends, journalist friends, people from all walks of life."

And she adds, "Here you are appreciated for what you are and not judged by how old you are."

AMY TONNESSEN is a Peace Corps volunteer in Pulawy, Poland, a large agricultural town on the Vistula River 120 kilometers from Warsaw. Winter comes early in this northern latitude, and many of the days are gloomy and cold. "I come from Florida where I see sunshine every day," Amy tells you. "I left Miami in eighty-degree weather and arrived in Pulawy on a bleak November afternoon.

Getting used to winter days here, when the sun sets at four o'clock, hasn't been easy."

But Amy has not let climate stop her from doing the job she came to Poland to do. She has a bachelor's degree in business from the University of Texas and an MBA (Master of Business Administration) degree from Rollins College in Orlando, Florida. Before joining the Peace Corps she was vice president for finance in a large Florida real estate company. Her assignment in Pulawy calls for her to work with local citizens who want to start private small businesses. That is no small task in a country that was under Communist control from the end of World War II until 1989. For almost fifty years there was no such thing as private enterprise. All business, big and small, was run by the government.

Amy's job is to help the prospective businessmen and businesswomen of Pulawy solve problems: what kind of business to start, how to get a loan, how to find a market. Her training and experience in the United States have equipped her to deal with such problems and many others. In order to be helpful in this new setting, her first task was to learn about local conditions and a bureaucracy that is still formidable, even though it is no longer Communist.

"A farmer came in wanting to grow hops for beer," Amy says by way of explanation, "but he had to have a loan to get started. I helped him cut through the red tape to get it, learning myself every step of the way. Another man who had worked for a while in the United States came in with all kinds of ideas based on what he had seen there. He wanted to open a gas station, a hotel, a grocery, maybe even a pizza place. His ideas were a jumble, and I've tried to help him focus on what he's best able to do."

Amy plans to start a small business incubator where people with hopes and problems can share office space, a computer, a fax machine, and other equipment at the same time they are getting advice.

Amy Tonnessen still attracts attention when she jogs in Pulawy.

One of Amy's successful projects was helping Pulawy take part in a large trade fair in the city of Poznan, where forty Polish towns and cities set up exhibits in order to attract investors.

Amy is happy in her assignment and says, "These are two years I'll never forget. I'm much more open to new ideas and different people. I've learned to do without things I used to think were necessities. My life has definitely taken a different path, thanks to the Peace Corps."

And Amy adds with a laugh, "Sometimes I surprise the people in Pulawy. Jogging is my hobby. You should see the stares I get. People here are not accustomed to seeing a person running down the street unless someone is chasing them."

TODAY over five hundred Peace Corps volunteers like Tom Ritter, Janice Hemphill, and Amy Tonnessen are at work in formerly Communist countries in Eastern Europe that until a few years ago were satellites of the Soviet Union, America's bitter political enemy. The volunteers in Europe are pioneering a new frontier for the Peace Corps, which for over thirty years had programs only in developing countries in Africa, Asia, Latin America, and in the Pacific and Caribbean areas. Why has the Peace Corps gone to these European countries that for almost half a century were shut off behind the Iron Curtain? What do the Peace Corps volunteers hope to accomplish there? What does the United States hope to accomplish by having them there?

In the pages ahead we will look closely at this new Peace Corps frontier and at what it says about our country. But to understand more fully why the Peace Corps is in Europe today, we need first to look at the birth and growth of this uniquely American institution.

IN THE early morning hours of October 14, 1960, John F. Kennedy spoke his first words about a Peace Corps. Then a Massachusetts senator and in a close presidential race against Vice President Richard Nixon, Kennedy was running very late when he reached the University of Michigan campus at Ann Arbor for a campaign speech. Although it was well past midnight, Kennedy and his aides were astonished to find that over ten thousand students were still waiting to hear him speak. Making his way to the Student Union Building and standing on the steps there, Kennedy spoke without notes and put his thoughts in the form of questions to the students. He asked how many of them would be willing to give up a part of their lives to work in Africa, Asia, and Latin America for the good of the people in those places and as a service to the United States. He asked whether they would be willing to contribute two years or more to the betterment of the poor countries of the world.

And speaking of the United States, he said, " . . . on your willingness to contribute part of your life to this country, I think, will depend the answer whether we as a free society can compete."

Two weeks later, in a major address at the Cow Palace in San Francisco, Kennedy put on record his intention to create a Peace Corps if he were elected president. The Peace Corps had now become a Kennedy campaign pledge and thus a campaign issue. Richard Nixon attacked the idea, calling it "superficial" and "conceived solely for campaign purposes."

But Nixon was wrong. Kennedy won the election and in his inaugural address on January 20, 1961, spoke the memorable words, "Ask not what your country can do for you. Ask what you can do for your country." Clearly, the thoughts he had shared with the University of Michigan students three months earlier were still very much on the new president's mind.

Moving swiftly, President Kennedy created the Peace Corps by executive order on March 1, less than six weeks after taking office. The guidelines for the new agency were clearly stated:

A Peace Corps volunteer goes to work with high school students in a vocational agriculture program in Pakistan, 1963.

The Peace Corps would be made up of volunteers who would receive no salary, only a modest living allowance.

Volunteers would be well qualified for the work they were sent to do.

They would live among the people they were sent to help, in villages or wherever else it might be, with no special housing or other privileges.

They would serve for two years, a period that could be extended if everyone agreed.

Kennedy asked Congress to make this new kind of national service a permanent government program, and within a few months the Senate and House of Representatives passed a Peace Corps Act by a large majority. In the Peace Corps Act, Congress stated with brevity and clarity that the purpose of the Peace Corps was to "promote world peace and friendship" by (1) helping developing countries meet their needs for trained workers, (2) furthering a better understanding of the American people on the part of the people served, (3) increasing America's understanding of other people.

A selection process was set up to screen the thousands of applicants for the Peace Corps and pick those best qualified for particular assignments. Training programs were established at a number of universities and colleges throughout the country.

By the end of 1961 five hundred volunteers had finished training and had begun work in nine widely scattered countries in Africa, Asia, and the Caribbean. During each of the next four years the Peace Corps increased in size and in the number of countries in which volunteers were serving. At the peak of its growth in 1966 almost sixteen thousand volunteers were at work in fifty-nine countries. In these early years of the Peace Corps' life the American people were intensely interested in what the volunteers were doing overseas. Newspapers, magazines, and television carried frequent

A Peace Corps volunteer helps build an A-frame school in the West African country of Sierra Leone, 1968.

human interest stories about what their lives in the developing world were like and what they were accomplishing.

Stories from the African country of Malawi recounted the work of volunteers in diagnosing tuberculosis in one thousand villagers and beginning treatment for them. A magazine article told how a volunteer in Pakistan led a thousand villagers in building earthen dams that saved rice crops in several villages from monsoon floods. Another story detailed the efforts of a few volunteers in the Phil-

13

A Peace Corps volunteer nurse at the Government Mental Hospital in Lahore, Pakistan, 1963.

ippines who organized a summer camp called Camp Brotherhood for six hundred needy children from the slums of Manila and other Philippine cities.

Such stories were true, but they were not typical of the experiences of most Peace Corps volunteers. Over half of all volunteers taught English, mathematics, and science, usually in isolated hinterland schools. Others worked in village community development where any progress was hard to see and in nurse training in poorly equipped provincial hospitals. Their jobs were sometimes dull, often frustrating. Almost without exception they faced times of loneliness, and in some cases their living conditions were marginal at best. Some volunteers wondered whether they were making any contribution. Some quit before their two-year assignments were completed. But most stayed on the job, did good work, and came to know the people of their host countries in a deep and personal way.

After 1966 the size of the Peace Corps began to decline as public attention focused on the Vietnam War and many Americans began to question U.S. involvement in world problems. During the seventies the Peace Corps received such limited publicity that some Americans thought it no longer existed. But they were wrong. Every president after Kennedy, including Richard Nixon, retained the Peace Corps as part of his administration and gave it unqualified support. The number of volunteers leveled out at five thousand to six thousand a year during the 1970s and 1980s, but programs—even though smaller—continued in a growing number of African, Asian, and Latin American countries.

Twenty-nine countries have had a Peace Corps program for twenty-five or more years. Some of the countries are Ecuador, Ghana, Jamaica, Nepal, the Philippines, and Thailand.

The Peace Corps entered the decade of the nineties with confidence, strength, and vigor. Volunteers are now serving in more than seventy countries in Africa, Asia, Latin America, and the Caribbean and Pacific areas. Congress has called for an increase in volunteer numbers to ten thousand by 1997.

In many ways the Peace Corps remains the same today as it was in its formative years. Volunteers are still carefully selected from thousands of applicants and serve two-year assignments. They receive about ten weeks of intensive training in the language and culture of the country to which they will be assigned. Education is still a major Peace Corps activity. Since 1961 over five million students in developing countries have been taught by Peace Corps volunteers.

There are some notable differences between the early Peace Corps and the Peace Corps of the nineties, however. In 1961 the average Peace Corps volunteer age was about twenty-four; today it is about thirty-one. One in ten volunteers today is fifty-five or older. The reason for the age change is that receiving countries today increasingly want volunteers with experience in technical fields such as fisheries development, forest and watershed management, primary health care systems, and teacher training. In the sixties most Peace Corps volunteers were men. Today men and women volunteers are about equal in number.

President Kennedy called the programs of his administration The New Frontier. The Peace Corps was on the cutting edge of the new frontier, and it has remained there.

2

Beyond the Cold War:
The Peace Corps
Goes to Europe

David Billet, from Los Angeles, one of the first Peace Corps volunteers in Hungary, teaching English in a suburban Budapest school.

DURING World War II the United States and Russia were allies, and a promising friendship seemed to be developing. In the final savage months of fighting, the United States and Britain liberated France, Belgium, the Netherlands, and other countries in Western and Northern Europe that Hitler's armies had ruthlessly overrun. Russia drove the German war machine out of Poland, the Baltic States, Czechoslovakia, Bulgaria, and other Eastern European nations. The Russians and their Western allies met in Germany; the Russians occupied the eastern part of the country, United States and British forces the western portion. The German capital city of Berlin, located in the east, was divided into British, French, and American occupation zones and a Russian sector.

Quickly, however, all hope of continued cooperation and friendship vanished. The Soviet Union, of which Russia was the dominant country, had no intention of pulling its troops out of the occupied countries of Eastern Europe until puppet Communist governments had been installed. Very quickly Poland, Czechoslovakia, Bulgaria, Romania, and Hungary became Russian satellites. The Baltic countries of Estonia, Latvia, and Lithuania were arbitrarily absorbed into the Soviet Union. All hope of German reunification disappeared in 1949 when East Germany, still occupied by Soviet troops, declared itself the German Democratic Republic with a Communist government firmly in place.

In 1948 the United States launched the European Recovery Program, called the Marshall Plan because George C. Marshall, the famous World War II general and later secretary of state, helped to conceive and administer it. Over $13 billion in American development aid poured into Great Britain, France, West Germany, and several other western and northern European democracies. The Marshall Plan was spectacularly successful in speeding the recovery of these war-ravished countries. Russia, however, kept Poland, Czechoslovakia, Romania, and its other European satellites from participating in the Marshall Plan. As a result, those countries lagged far behind in returning to economic health. It was at this time that Churchill coined the famous phrase "Iron Curtain" to describe the closing off of the Communist countries of Europe from the free world.

Tension between the superpowers reached a dangerous level when the Soviets shut off American, British, and French access to West Berlin by a land and water blockade. The Western Allies resorted to a massive airlift to transport supplies to West Berlin. After lengthy negotiations, Russia cancelled the blockade, but the pattern of noncooperation and outright hostility between Communist and democratic nations was now set. This grim ideological, political, and economic conflict spread to Africa, Asia, and other parts of the world and became known as the Cold War.

THE Peace Corps was born in the depths of the Cold War. The first group of Peace Corps volunteers in 1961 began their service in

Africa at the same time the Communist government of East Germany built the wall to seal off East Berlin from West Berlin. More than anything else, the Berlin Wall became the symbol of the Cold War.

The Communist propaganda machine in Moscow lost no time in trying to convince all African, Asian, and Latin American countries that the Peace Corps was an organization of spies and evil agents of capitalism. Soviet publications began to refer to the Peace Corps as the "Spy Corps" and called it "an instrument of American imperialism." Russian anti-Peace Corps propaganda could be low-key and cleverly written, but it could also be wildly ludicrous. One Soviet pamphlet said that "Peace Corps candidates are rejected if they miss a nickel at fifty yards with a Colt revolver." A Communist periodical in India published a series of lurid articles accusing Peace Corps volunteers of spreading diseases among the poultry flocks of poor Indian farmers.

The able civil servants in charge of Peace Corps programs for the receiving countries were well aware that the Peace Corps had no connections with U.S. intelligence agencies and saw through Soviet attacks on the Peace Corps. With only a few exceptions, Communist propaganda was only a minor irritant for volunteers once they had established themselves in the community where they were working.

COMMUNIST rule in Eastern Europe collapsed in 1989. With a speed that astonished and shocked the rest of the world, one European country after another made the first critical moves to throw off the yoke of communism and move toward a democratic form of government. In Poland, the reform-minded Solidarity labor union and political movement, outlawed in 1981, was again legalized; in June elections, Solidarity and its political allies won control of the parliament. In October the Communist party in Hungary abolished itself and called for free elections. With dizzying swiftness in November and December, Communist party leaders in Czechoslovakia, Bulgaria, Romania, and East Germany either resigned or were overthrown. On November 9 the Berlin Wall was destroyed, and German unification was only months away. In all of these countries, forty years of domination by the Soviet Union had ended.

Most of the dramatic changes in the Eastern European countries seemed to happen almost overnight, but in fact they had been in the making for a long time. Although Russia had imposed communism on its neighbors immediately after World War II, it had never succeeded in suppressing a desire for democracy. Demands for democratic reforms resulted in riots and public protests in Hungary in 1956, Czechoslovakia in 1968, and Poland in 1981. With troops and tanks, the Soviet Union ruthlessly put down these popular movements, but it could not kill the spirit behind them. Even though outlawed, the Solidarity movement in Poland stayed alive, and leaders such as Lech Walesa in Poland and Vaclav Havel in Czechoslovakia kept hope for democratic reform alive. Even younger Communist party leaders in some of the satellite countries knew that reforms were necessary.

In the Soviet Union itself a major Communist party crisis was coming to a head, brought on by decades of political favoritism, governmental inefficiency and graft, unequal distribution of goods and services, excessive military spending, environmental pollution, and economic stagnation. When Poland, Czechoslovakia, and the other Soviet satellite countries revolted, their giant Communist master was helpless to intervene as it had in the past. Communism as a political philosophy had been discredited, and the Soviet Union itself was crumbling.

SUDDENLY the Cold War was over, and the countries of Eastern Europe shut off behind the Iron Curtain for over four decades were able to look out, to reach out, to communicate. Here were countries with rich, ancient cultures that had produced great leaders and great music, literature, and architecture. Now they needed financial assistance to rebuild their ruined economies and severely damaged environments. They needed to rebuild their knowledge of the free-enterprise system. They needed fresh ideas and the tools to communicate with a world they hardly knew. These countries that Russia had kept from taking part in the Marshall Plan almost half a century earlier now desperately needed that kind of economic recovery help. Although momentarily stunned by the speed with which communism had collapsed, the United States and the western European democracies prepared to respond.

Ambassador Mark Palmer, the American ambassador in Hungary, knew very well about the need of Hungary and the other formerly Communist countries for financial help. He also knew that other kinds of help were needed, and the idea came to him that the Peace Corps might be able to make a contribution in meeting some of those needs. English teaching and learning had been a limited and suspect activity in the Communist world for many years. The Russians had promoted their own language everywhere they could, and Russian was the most widely spoken and understood language in all former satellite countries. The dramatic political change and the need and overwhelming desire to join the global community triggered an explosion of interest in English.

Peace Corps volunteers had proved in a hundred countries around the world that they were good English teachers. Ambassador Palmer was also sure that volunteers could be recruited to help with environmental problems and in introducing private business knowledge and skills that had had no place in the Communist ideology. Volunteers could bring energy, spirit, and fresh ideas to countries that needed all those things. And of great importance: volunteers could learn about the people and the countries so long shut off

Michael Eyres teaches English at a high school in Warsaw. "It's been good," he says of his Peace Corps service. "If I had the decision to make again, I would do the same thing. Being a Peace Corps volunteer has let me see the world." Michael plans to continue teaching when he returns to the United States.

behind the Iron Curtain and bring their knowledge back to America.

When Ambassador Palmer raised the possibility of a Peace Corps program with Hungarian officials, he found strong interest. The Peace Corps then sent senior Washington staff member Jon Keeton to Hungary to further explore a possible program. Soon after arriving in the capital city of Budapest, he met with the Hungarian minister of education. The minister did not mince words. He told Keeton that his country was determined to replace Russian with English as its primary foreign language. He said Hungary wanted ten thousand Peace Corps volunteers to teach English.

When Keeton recovered from the shock, he told the minister that no program of that size was possible (at that time the Peace Corps worldwide numbered about six thousand volunteers) but that a small program that could grow larger over the years was possible. Keeton made his visit in late June. A few days later President George Bush visited some of the Eastern European countries, the first U.S. president to do so since the early days of the Cold War. On July 12 in a speech in Budapest, the president announced that the Peace Corps would establish a new program in Hungary.

Immediately inquiries about the Peace Corps began to come in from other formerly Communist countries of Europe. Poland also asked for ten thousand Peace Corps English teachers! Czechoslovakia was quick to express its interest in receiving Peace Corps volunteers. The American ambassador in Czechoslovakia at that time was Shirley Temple Black, who in earlier life had been America's most famous child movie star. Mrs. Black had previously been ambassador to the West African country of Ghana and had known many Peace Corps volunteers there. Now she expressed her belief that volunteers could make unique and valuable contributions to Czechoslovakia.

The prospect of Peace Corps programs in Eastern Europe aroused tremendous interest in the United States, but questions were also raised. Why be eager to help countries that so recently had been our enemies or at least friends of our enemies? Some members of Congress pointed out that for thirty years the Peace Corps had worked only in the developing countries of Africa, Asia, Latin America, and the Pacific and Caribbean areas. They asked if that was not the Peace Corps' real mission. Some former Peace Corps volunteers who had worked in the Third World countries expressed their concern that programs in Europe would drain money and volunteers away from the poor parts of the world that still needed the most help.

Peace Corps officials in Washington assured both Congress and returned volunteers that programs in Europe would not mean diminished concern for traditional Third World programs. They also pointed out that the Peace Corps Act does not limit volunteers to Africa, Asia, and Latin America. The Peace Corps' position, officials reminded critics, has always been that volunteers can be sent to any country where they are wanted and needed and where conditions are such that they can work effectively. That description fits all of the formerly Communist countries of Eastern Europe.

On June 15, 1990, President Bush met with 121 volunteers in a White House Rose Garden ceremony to mark the historic occasion of their departure for Europe. The next day sixty-one Hungary volunteers arrived in Budapest. On June 18 sixty volunteers for Poland touched down at Warsaw's International Airport. The Peace Corps had come to Europe.

3

The Peace Corps
in Poland

Peace Corps volunteer Julia Jowers (standing) with a Polish staff member of the Ecology and Health Foundation in Warsaw, where Julia works. Julia, a native of Austin, Texas, has a master's degree in environmental studies. "I'm very excited about a project we've just started," Julia says. "It is a preliminary look at lead levels in children. We will take blood samples from three hundred children and send them to the Communicable Disease Center in Atlanta. From there we will launch a full-scale program to educate mothers."

POLAND is located in the heart of Europe. With an area of 120,000 square miles, it is about the size of Arkansas and Missouri combined; its population of forty million makes it the largest of the Eastern European countries that were satellites of the Soviet Union. With a national history that dates from the tenth century, Poland has produced men and women who have left their mark on the world: Copernicus, the founder of modern astronomy; Madame Curie, twice a Nobel Prize winner for chemistry research; Ignace Paderewski, great pianist and statesman; Chopin; Pope John Paul II, to name only a few of the most famous.

With Germany on its western border and Russia on its eastern border, Poland was caught in a deadly World War II vice. The war was triggered by Germany's unprovoked invasion of Poland on September 1, 1939. Seventeen days later, Russia (at that time allied with Germany) invaded from the east, and the helpless country was divided between the two super military powers. When Germany broke the alliance and attacked Russia in 1941, all of Poland was seized by Germany.

For the next three years the Polish people endured forced labor, starvation, massacres, and infamous concentration camps such as Auschwitz. An estimated six million Poles were killed, half of them Jews. Throughout these years of horror, the Polish resistance movement and strong underground organizations never died out. In 1944 the people of Warsaw joined with the underground Home Army and rose up against the German occupiers in a courageous effort to drive them from the city. For sixty-three days they fought in their homes and in barricaded streets before finally being defeated by the overwhelming superiority of Nazi guns and tanks. In his fury, Hitler ordered the complete destruction of Warsaw. While about 15 percent of the buildings survived, no other city in Europe suffered the degree of devastation that befell Warsaw. Over 200,000 Poles died in the Warsaw uprising, and those who survived were ordered out of the city.

After World War II the Polish people rebuilt their cities and country as best they could under the constraints of the Communist system imposed by the Soviets. Now that it has toppled the Communist regime, Poland faces monumental tasks of government reform and of reviving a desperately depressed economy: solving international currency problems, ending government monopolies and creating a private business sector, building commercial distribution systems, creating a banking system. The list seems endless.

The Peace Corps program in Poland is now the largest in Europe. Volunteers are teaching English, working in small business development, and helping with environmental problems. Their qualifications are outstanding. The small business volunteers have had years of experience running businesses, working on Wall Street, teaching in universities. Eighty-five percent of the English teachers have masters or Ph.D. degrees, and they average over nine years of teaching experience.

In a country with so many needs, the Peace Corps contribution

Peace Corps volunteer Mary Nolan teaches English at the National School of Public Administration in Warsaw. She thinks she will extend her service for a third year. "I have given up too much to just be here two years," she says. "I gave up a beautiful little home in San Francisco and my two cats. My investment in Poland is too great for so short a time." And Mary adds, "I'll come out a changed person. There's no doubt I'll receive more than I'll give."

may seem small, but it can still be important. Already volunteers have been of major help in the opening of forty-eight new teacher training colleges in Poland. In some cases individual volunteers make outstanding contributions. Volunteer Jean Zukowski-Faust, for example, received the Polish National Medal of Education for helping to design the curriculum for the colleges and for organizing the donation of one million books to Polish schools from American publishers. Bill Grant, a volunteer from Atlanta, organized two highly successful national workshops on setting up and running banks in Poland.

Timothy Carroll is director of the Peace Corps program in Poland. "Volunteers are wanted," he says. "The people want to be helped."

And Carroll makes another point. "There has been a long love affair between Poland and America. One fourth of the population has an American relative with whom they are in touch."

"They Want Perfection"

"THESE students demand a lot. They want perfection."

The speaker is Stephen Springer, a Peace Corps volunteer from Atlanta, and he is talking about the men and women he teaches at the National School of Public Administration in Warsaw. The school may be the most prestigious educational institution in Poland because it was created by the Parliament of the Republic of Poland and attached to the office of the prime minister. The director is a distinguished law professor, but the prime minister gives the school his personal supervision.

The National School of Public Administration was created in 1991, two years after the Communist government was voted out of existence. Its purpose is no less than to train senior civil servants who will replace the old guard Soviet-oriented officials and undo the Communist policies of forty years. The new civil servants will be expected to bring about reform that will—to quote the school's own charter—make possible the growth of an "efficient, modern country."

Students are chosen for the National School of Public Administration with the utmost care. Even to apply, a person must be no older than thirty, have a college or university degree, and have a good knowledge of English, French, or German. All applicants must already have done well in some field such as teaching. Applicants go through a series of competitive examinations, and eventually only about one out of ten is admitted to the school. Among many other things, the two-year program covers public law and administration, economics, public finance, international public relations, and international law.

"The government is making a huge investment in these people," Steve Springer says, "and expects a great deal from them. When they finish this program, they're guaranteed high-level positions."

When it turned to the Peace Corps for help in staffing the school, the prime minister's office expected a great deal. In Steve Springer it got exactly what it wanted. Steve is thirty-three and has both a law degree and a master's degree in American Studies from the University of Alabama. He taught in the university's law school and business school for two-and-half years before joining the Peace Corps.

About his reasons for becoming a Peace Corps volunteer, Steve says, "While I was still in law school, I realized I wanted to be a teacher, and I knew I would need a Ph.D. Before I started a doctoral program, I had to have a change. Peace Corps is my period of change. I told myself I would learn a lot from living and teaching in another culture, and I have."

Steve teaches several classes each day, Monday through Friday, at the National School of Public Administration. Each class is limited to eight students, making possible a great deal of give and take between teacher and students. They already have a working knowledge of English, but they want much more than that.

"They want to know professional English," Steve says, "the English of business, the English of law. They want to know American slang. They are always asking about what Americans think and do. We talk about such things as discrimination against minorities, discrimination against women. I have two outspoken women students in one class who love it."

Steve continues, "Everyone in Warsaw wants to learn English. Lots of kids learn it from listening to American songs. We volunteers laugh among ourselves. If the Peace Corps fires us, we can make a lot more money by private tutoring. In an hour we could make twice our daily Peace Corps allowance. Lots of people have offered to pay us for tutoring and are puzzled when we tell them we can't earn money.

"It's rather nice not to have to worry about charging. We can tutor whomever we like. That's why we started the 'English Underground'—that's our weekly English class located in the basement of our hostel. We collected everybody who had asked us to tutor them, and we give them free English lessons."

Steve has a tiny suite of rooms in the hostel where his students live. The hostel is located dead center in the old Jewish ghetto, on a street where during World War II Jews were loaded into trucks for trips to the death camps. This part of Warsaw, totally laid waste at the end of the war, is today a bustling area of apartment buildings and little shops. But a nearby monument to the valor of those who died in the Warsaw uprising of 1944 reminds all who see it of the city's courageous and tragic past.

Peace Corps volunteers receive about ten weeks of training before they begin their work. In the early sixties most training took place on American university campuses, but now volunteers are given all of their training in the country in which they will serve. In most cases they live with "host families" so that they will hear the local language day and night, eat the food of the people, and learn the customs of the country through everyday living. The Peace Corps staff in the country arranges for the host families and also brings the trainees together regularly for language classes and study of the customs, traditions, history, and government of the country.

Steve lived with a Polish family for part of his training, but he also spent some time living with two university teachers. "I still can't believe how hard the Polish language is," Steve will tell you. "After studying the language half a day for ten weeks, what I know is a drop in the bucket. I can ask directions, shop in the market, figure out street signs, say polite things. But really learning to use the language is just a long, slow process.

"And learning about the country," Steve continues. "That starts in training and keeps right on going. Things don't run smoothly here. Something that would take five minutes at home—like getting a monthly bus pass—can take all day in Warsaw. Opening an account in a bank here is a bureaucratic nightmare. It's hard to believe."

Steve knows that these kinds of problems are largely a hangover from the old Communist bureaucracy. He knows that the kind of civil servant managers now being trained at the National School of Public Administration will be expected to bring changes in all levels of government that will end these nightmares. And Steve also knows that the main purpose of his being in Poland is to bring a few fresh ideas that may help in solving problems.

Steve's living quarters are provided by the school, and he receives a living allowance of $200 a month from the Peace Corps—a small fraction of what he would be earning in the United States if he had

With his limited Peace Corps living allowance, Steve Springer has learned to be a careful shopper in a Warsaw neighborhood market.

not decided to join the Peace Corps. "We can get by," Steve says, speaking of himself and other volunteers, "but we have to be careful. Eating out is expensive. I do all of my cooking on a one-element hot plate, so my meals are pretty basic. I eat a lot of Polish sandwiches: a slice of bread, cheese, and a slice of tomato. Prices fluctuate wildly. Last week the price of cucumbers went up 400 percent."

Steve has become good at shopping in the immense outdoor market near his hostel and discussing prices has been very good for his Polish. He takes his time, wandering slowly through the scores of stalls. He buys bread at one, kasha at another, potatoes and carrots and a rare expensive apple at a third. He carefully pulls off bills from his little roll, watching every *zloti* (the denomination of Polish currency).

As Steve looks out over the bewildering jumble of little market stalls, he says, "My host family visited the States once very briefly. The thing that impressed them most out of everything they saw was the supermarket, a place where they could buy everything under one roof. I can see why now."

"I Want Things to Keep Going after I've Gone"

WHEN a country needs something and a Peace Corps volunteer has what it takes to meet that need, the result should be a perfect assignment. Paul Braun would not call his assignment in Poland's Kampinos National Park perfect, not by a long shot, but he will acknowledge that it might be as good as it gets in the real world.

"They do need me here," Paul says with no false modesty. "They need my computer experience."

Paul, who is twenty-six, comes from Genesee Depot, Wisconsin, and has a degree in landscape architecture from the University of Wisconsin. Before joining the Peace Corps, Paul was the computer expert for the state of Wisconsin's department of natural resources. Working in the program of water regulation and zoning, he computerized maps of all of the wetlands in the state so that they could be more efficiently monitored.

The Polish government asked the Peace Corps for someone who could do a similar job for Kampinos National Park, and the Peace Corps selected Paul Braun. With eighty thousand acres, Kampinos National Park is the largest park in Poland, and—quite astonishingly—it is located on the very edge of Warsaw. It is the largest national park in Europe that is near a major city. Because of its closeness to Warsaw, Kampinos has an unusually large number of visitors year round.

Timothy Carroll, the Peace Corps director in Poland, is sure that the heavy visitor volume can be explained in part by the way the people of Warsaw had to exist under communism. He explains, "Families, for decades, have only been permitted to have a regulated minimum square footage of living space, but rather than submit to this cramped condition, Poles have become an outdoor people, enjoying their garden plots and their parks in every kind of weather."

Paul agrees. "Every Pole I've met says he comes here to hike, picnic, or cross-country ski."

As wonderful as the Kampinos location is for the people of Warsaw and other nearby towns and cities, the park itself pays a heavy price. "The park is hard to manage," Paul says. "It is part of six counties, each with its own government. None of them has a landfill, so lots of people drive a little way into the park and dump their garbage. Poaching is a problem, especially poaching of deer and fox. When the park was formed, a number of farms and villages were included; about two thousand people still live in the park.

Paul Braun at work in Kampinos National Park near Warsaw.

That's a problem. How do you preserve nature and meet the needs of communities at the same time?"

Kampinos National Park has within its boundaries a wide variety of terrain: inland dunes covered with forests, marshes, meadows, farmland, and wasteland. Forests cover almost three-fourths of the area. The Vistula River flows on the park's edge, giving life to small rivers, sandy islands, and willow clumps. These areas are important habitats for bird life. The park is home for 160 species of birds, among them the black stork, cranes, peregrine falcon, and marsh harrier. About five thousand species of fauna are found in the park—among the most interesting are the European elk and wild boar—and over one thousand species of vascular plants. Eighty-one species of endangered animals live in the park. Winding through the forests and dunes are 225 miles of tourist trails.

"Kampinos is a great natural treasure for Poland," Paul says. "It needs a twenty-year land-use management plan. It needs a tourist management plan. It has to have an environmental education plan. To plan you have to know what is here, how much is here, and where it is, and you have to put that information in the computer so you can use it. I'm here to help with that."

But when Paul arrived at Kampinos National Park after finishing his training, he found one of those "real world" situations that keeps any assignment from being perfect. The job was there, he was there—but there was no money to carry out the work! Somehow when the park's budget for the year had been figured, no one had remembered to put in a line item for computerized mapping. While money was being found—a bureaucratic task that took several months—Paul occupied himself with miscellaneous park jobs, but he did put some of the time to very good use. He had brought a mountain bike from home, and with a Polish colleague, he explored every trail in the park and gained a better understanding of Kampinos in its vast entirety.

"And," Paul says with some satisfaction, "when I look at a map, when I work with the maps, I know what the park is really like. I've been all over it."

Paul expresses his personal motives very simply: "I want things to keep going after I'm gone."

Finally, money for his work was put in the budget, and Paul is now busily engaged in his computerized mapping and in organizing a mountain of information about the park. Creating geographic information systems will make possible management and analysis techniques that were until now impossible. Kampinos National Park can become a model and training center for Poland's seventeen other national parks.

Paul's only regret now is that he no longer has time to be outdoors in the park as much as he would like to be. "It's something I really love. Walking home last week, I collected mushrooms and wound up with fifteen varieties."

Home for Paul is a forester's house where he lives with a park worker and his family. "A Polish family is so hospitable," Paul says. "They make you feel part of their family. They overfeed you, of course, and go to great lengths to make you comfortable."

4

The Peace Corps in the Czech Republic and Slovakia

"The salvation of our world

can be found only in the human heart."

Vaclav Havel, first president of Czechoslovakia
after free elections in 1990

CZECHOSLOVAKIA, the country to which the Peace Corps sent volunteers in 1989, no longer exists. At the stroke of midnight December 31, 1992, the union of the Czech and Slovak people that created Czechoslovakia after World War I was dissolved in a quiet ceremony. On January 1, Europe had two new independent countries, the Czech Republic and Slovakia. Unlike the horror of Serbians against Bosnians in Yugoslavia, the separation of Czechs and Slovaks was entirely peaceful. Still, the breakup was yet another example of old ethnic rivalries causing trouble and preventing cooperation in Europe. The two ethnic groups that had maintained their unity so courageously to overcome the Soviet Union could not stay together once the Communist menace was removed.

The breakup caused no problems for the ninety Peace Corps volunteers in Czechoslovakia at the time it became two countries. They had been welcome in Czechoslovakia. "I've never been in a more pro-American country," said Stephen Hanchey, director of the Peace Corps program in Czechoslovakia. The volunteers continued to be welcome in the Czech Republic and Slovakia. A priority objective of both countries is to replace most teaching of Russian with the teaching of English. Peace Corps volunteers were helping to do that in Czechoslovakia. The countries they are now in have different names, but the volunteers' work is the same.

Yet these volunteers will return to America after two years with the memory that the country they went to serve broke apart while they were there. One of the Peace Corps' objectives is for volunteers to learn from their foreign experiences and to bring what they have learned back with them. The volunteers who went to Czechoslovakia will have learned a sobering lesson about the poison of ethnic hatred.

The Black Triangle of Death

THE traveler in the Czech Republic and Slovakia will soon fall under the spell of the beauty and variety of the landscape, especially in spring when flowers bloom on every hillside and fruit trees are in blossom in every valley. The agricultural plains are yellow with fields of mustard, green with young wheat and corn. Along lakes and rivers—the Elbe, the Danube—one sees forests and recreational areas for summer vacationers. Castles, as many as three thousand and some still inhabited, rise dramatically from hilltops.

But beneath this beauty and sometimes side by side with it, environmental damage has been in progress for decades. Under the Communist system, industrial production was pushed with little or no pollution control. In some areas factories and mines discharge chemical wastes into rivers. Lead, fluorine gas, and cadmium dust spew into the air continually. In many places environmental damage is not visible, but chemical fertilizers used to increase agricultural production have contaminated the soil and ground and surface water.

A pamphlet issued by the Federal Committee for the Environment, Czech and Slovakia republics, contains this statement:

Environmental damage has affected human, animal, and plant life in many ways. One-third of the forests have been destroyed. Over half of the fish and other vertebrate species are endangered. High levels of lead have been found in the blood of children, mainly in the more polluted areas. Respiratory and heart diseases, along with various forms of cancer, are the main illnesses and causes of death, especially in the industrial areas. Life expectancy, especially among males, is several years less than in Western countries.

After the Communists were turned out of power in November, 1989, the new Czechoslovakian government immediately created three separate ministries to study the magnitude of environmental damage and to develop laws and plans for attacking the terrible problems. The fight will be long and costly and painful to those who lose jobs when inefficient and hazardous factories and mines are closed.

The Czech Republic and Slovakia, as well as other Eastern European countries, have a number of small private organizations (called NGOS or Non-Government Organizations) that were agitating for environmental reforms years before the government became interested. They also carry out programs of health and environmental education for the general public and schools. Peace Corps volunteers have been requested by most Eastern European countries to work with the NGOS.

David Lowrence is an environmental volunteer assigned to work with two NGOS in the Czech Republic. At twenty-three, David is one of the younger Peace Corps volunteers in Eastern Europe. Since

David Lowrence.

most of the environment activists in the European countries emerging from communism are young men and women, David fits in very well. He is also well qualified, with a bachelor's degree in biology and environmental studies from Tufts University in Massachusetts. He was class salutatorian and remembers that he mentioned the Peace Corps in his speech.

About his joining the Peace Corps, David says, "When I heard of the new programs in Eastern Europe, the prospect of witnessing democratic change was irresistible, plus, of course, the chance to do something about a badly damaged environment. My motives for becoming a volunteer were a combination of altruism and self-interest, which is healthy, I think. It was an opportunity to get valuable experience before going to graduate school and at the same time to help these countries at a time when they need help most. And also help break down the ridiculous barriers that have separated us."

In the capital city of Prague, where David lives, he works three days a week with an NGO called the Czech Union of Nature Protectors; as its name suggests, its mission is to promote policies which will lead to better forest management, soil conservation, animal protection, and other environmental concerns. David's specific job is to review all Czech-produced films on the environment and health education, catalog them, and develop a plan for their most effective distribution around the country.

The other two days of the workweek David travels by bus to Most, a city of about eighty thousand, a two-hour ride from Prague. For most of the journey the bus traverses the gently rolling landscape of northern Bohemia with its tidy villages, orchards, and richly fertile, highly cultivated fields. Then suddenly, as the bus approaches Most, this beauty gives way to an expanse of belching smokestacks and dead forests. This, David soon learned, is part of the most seriously degraded area in Europe—perhaps in the world—and takes in portions of southeast Saxony (Germany), Silesia (Poland), and northern Bohemia in the Czech Republic. This piece of geography that includes three countries is commonly called "the dirty triangle," but it is also known by a more dramatic name: the Black Triangle of Death.

Underlying this entire area are huge deposits of low-quality brown coal, which has a high sulfur content. Much of Eastern Europe's chemical, metallurgical, and heavy industry is packed into this area, and it is fueled by brown coal. Inefficient burning, poor technology, and a total disregard of environmental consequences on the part of the former Communist regime have created terrible problems of pollution. Large areas have been defaced by coal mining. Because of the insatiable demand for coal, the old section of Most and one hundred villages around the city have been swallowed up by open-pit mining.

"My first exposure to Litvinov, a small town near Most where I do part of my work, was on the worst sort of a day possible," David says. "Picture this setting: a chemical plant and an oil refinery, two coal-burning power plants, smoldering landfills. It was foggy, and we were in the middle of an inversion. On sulfur dioxide alert days like this school kids actually wear masks to protect them against the pollutants! I was shocked, truly shocked, when I saw this. I actually had a pain in my chest.

"I had always thought there would be certain conditions people would not tolerate without mass migration or revolution. I couldn't imagine that people would live under such conditions. I was wrong. Under the old Communist system workers were paid a 'death benefit.' Their salaries were four times greater than in the rest of the country. They would die sooner, but they had a job. The worker here will say, 'My children are unhealthy, I am unhealthy. But I need this job.' "

In this place David works with an NGO called Greenhouse

Litvinov. The work is not very satisfactory. "I guess you could call me their chief fund raiser," he said. "I would write letters to foreign organizations trying to get money for Greenhouse's projects. I didn't get much at first, but now I'm getting better. I am learning how to write a good grant proposal."

David also teaches environmental education at a junior high school near Most. "Environmental education courses usually are not much more than nature walks," he says. "Mine is different. We have the perfect laboratory right here. We talk about acid rain and the Greenhouse Effect and what is happening to the people and their country. Some of that will sink in, and maybe a few will decide to do something about it." David teaches his classes in the Czech language.

David is not happy with what he is accomplishing as a Peace Corps volunteer, but his unhappiness is less an indication of failure on his part than of the towering environmental problems facing not only the Czech Republic but all of Eastern Europe. He enjoys his teaching most. "Besides environment, we talk about sports and music and lots of other things," he says. "I like my kids a lot."

"Living Here Is a Great Adventure"

ANYONE meeting the Peace Corps volunteers serving in the ex-Communist countries of Eastern Europe is certain to be impressed by how well prepared, how well qualified, they are. Regardless of their age they are ambitious, high-achieving people with superior educations and a history of success in their work before they joined the Peace Corps.

In many ways Beth Klein is an example of everything the ideal Peace Corps volunteer should be. Beth teaches English in the small town of Rokycany in the western part of the Czech Republic. She is the only native speaker of English in town and is well on her way to mastering the Czech language. She has become a part of the community; when she walks down the street, people wave to her, stop to talk with her. She lives with a Czech family and has become comfortably a member of the household.

Beth is twenty-six, outgoing, of medium height, with brown eyes and glints of red in her brown hair. She earned a bachelor's degree in social science from Florida State University and a master's degree in social studies education at the University of Florida. After that she taught in a Florida high school for two years.

"My reasons for joining the Peace Corps aren't very original," Beth says, "the traditional urge to help others and a desire to travel. I wasn't tied down by possessions. I didn't own much of anything —a water bed and a dresser and books and clothes. It was a perfect time for me to go.

"I wasn't running away; I wasn't escaping something I disliked. My life in Florida was very satisfying. I had great students, a great boss, a nice place to live. But I think of Rokycany as my home now. Living here is a great adventure. I would like to stay here, and I may extend my Peace Corps assignment for a year. But eventually I want to go back and get my Ph.D."

The top 10 percent of the town's high school students attend the school where Beth teaches. It is a college preparatory school, and almost without exception her students will go to college. Beth attracts students like a magnet when she walks through the halls between classes. A tall, jean-clad boy with a safety pin for an earring stops her. They have a long conversation partly in English, partly in Czech. He tries to convince her—as he has for several days—to

Beth Klein talks with two of her students.

go to a heavy metal concert. Finally she laughs and agrees to go next week.

"I've had to work hard to get the kids and the other teachers to stop being shy and talk to me," Beth says. "In the past English has been taught here by reading only. They're not comfortable talking. At first I wondered why I was here. I hadn't come to teach beginners. I didn't realize how much they actually knew; they had a huge passive vocabulary which they never used. Slowly I have been uncovering it. I have forced them to bring it out and use it.

"In a way I'm an oddity because I make them do things other teachers don't. I ask them questions that make them use their imagination. I'll say, 'What would you do if you woke up one morning and your hair was green?' or 'What will you be doing ten years from now?' At first they would just say, 'I don't know.' Now they have learned to cope with my questions, and we have some funny, lively conversations in the classroom. One of my students, who has gone on to a university and whose English is fantastic, told me, 'You used to drive us crazy, but now I appreciate what you did for us.' "

Beth is in class twenty-four hours a week. In addition she is faculty adviser for three after-school language clubs. She also gives private English tutoring to adults and charges an hourly fee. Since Peace Corps volunteers aren't allowed to make money, Beth donates her tutoring fees to her school to buy English books.

Of her heavy schedule, she says, "Lots of students want help. I'm happiest when I'm overloaded. Four days a week, I walk home in the dark."

Beth leads an active, extremely full and varied life. She takes lessons on the classical guitar and gives English lessons in exchange. She is learning to knit. She has a small vegetable and flower garden in front of the house. She plays volleyball every Friday night. She has gone on white-water rafting and camping trips down nearby

Beth Klein with her Czech family, the Sysels.

rivers with her family and other friends. The family introduced her
to a local boating club, and she occasionally goes with twenty-five
or thirty other people on outdoor adventures.

"I have friends of all ages," Beth says, "from thirteen to sixty-
two. At home I wouldn't have that intergenerational experience."

The family Beth lives with, the Sysels, has an interesting makeup:
a grandmother, parents who are white-collar factory managers, and
their two daughters, ages eleven and eighteen. Also: two black cats,

a dog, and Corina, a Yugoslav turtle belonging to Hanina, the eleven-year-old. It is an active, outdoor-oriented family.

Says Hana, the mother, "It is good for the family to have Beth because it improves our English. But much more important: we didn't know much about Americans and how they live before Beth came. And we try to show her how normal Czechs live."

When an occasional American visits Beth in Rokycany, she may take the person to the main square and point out a wall on which has been mounted a small plaque. The plaque reads, "To Our Liberators, the 9th Infantry Regiment, 2nd Division, U.S. Army."

Beth explains, "Rokycany was the last city to be liberated by the Americans on this front during World War II. Everything east of here was freed by the Russians. Russian soldiers stopped on those hills over there and watched while our GI's drove the Germans out. The people here love us and accept us with open arms. Armistice Day is celebrated with a great display of American flags right here in this plaza."

And Beth adds, "They're going through a stage here now, after being force-fed Russian culture so long, where everything American is wonderful."

"You Have to Care More about Your Students Than Yourself"

OLOMOUC, about a hundred miles to the east of Prague, is an ancient city of spires and red roofs where one still encounters chimney sweeps walking down the street with their long brushes slung over their shoulders. Olomouc is located not far from one of Europe's most famous battle sites, Austerlitz, where Napoleon defeated

Ann Kurtz shopping in the Olomouc market. "Food is a problem in the winter," she says. "There are no fresh fruits or vegetables. We live on potatoes and bread and take vitamins." Ann cooks her meals on a two-burner hot plate in her room.

Students enjoy informal teatime chats with Ann.

combined forces of Russia and Austria. Tolstoy wrote eloquently about the battle in *War and Peace*.

History is everywhere in Olomouc. The building still stands where Mozart was confined with smallpox for six weeks after he had come to the city to perform. Not far away is a building where Lafayette was imprisoned. In another place is a monument erected by survivors of the Black Plague in the fourteenth century. The Russian army drove the Germans out of Olomouc at the end of World War II and stayed. Until the Czechs and Slovaks overcame the Communist regime in 1989, a large force of Russian troops was encamped just outside the city. Now it is gone.

In this historic city Peace Corps volunteer Ann Kurtz holds a position of unusual responsibility: the supervision of all second-year

English courses in the Philosophical Faculty of Palacky University. With seven thousand undergraduate students, Palacky University is the second largest institution of higher learning in the Czech Republic. It is also one of the most prestigious. Besides the Philosophical Faculty and the Divinity Faculty, Palacky has a medical college and a teachers' training college. Like the city of Olomouc itself, Palacky University has ancient roots: it had its beginning in 1566.

Why is a Peace Corps volunteer needed in such a distinguished university? The main reason is that the Russian army's occupation after the Czech revolt in 1968 and the following decades of Soviet domination caused great damage to the quality of education at Palacky, including training in the English language. The peaceful or "velvet" revolution that swept the Communists out of power in 1989 was the beginning of rebuilding for Palacky University. One move in their rebuilding was to ask the Peace Corps for help in revitalizing the teaching of English.

And how does it happen that a woman in her seventies, mother of two and grandmother of eight, should be given this heavy responsibility? Well, consider her background: She took her first degree from Wellesley College and then went on to earn a Ph.D. in German literature from the University of Maryland. During World War II she served in the navy at a secret communications center. After the war she taught at the University of Hawaii and the University of California at Santa Barbara. In the course of a long life in education, she has taught English in Tokyo, French and English in Iran, and German at the University of Dublin in Ireland. Along the way she was awarded five highly prized Fulbright grants, which provide for the exchange of students and teachers between the United States and other countries. Her last teaching post was at Meredith College in Raleigh, North Carolina, from which she retired at the age of seventy in 1991.

Margaret Russell with students at Palacky University. Margaret, who is sixty-three, works with Ann Kurtz at the university. Before coming to the Czech Republic, she taught high school English for twenty-five years in Kansas City, Missouri. "I dropped everything when the Peace Corps came along with its program in Europe," Margaret says, "and I like it."

But her retirement must have been one of the shortest on record. She applied to the Peace Corps almost immediately, and the Peace Corps saw in her just the person they needed for an important assignment in Europe. "I retired in May, and two months later I was in Olomouc," Ann says. "These European countries needed help, and Europe was the only place I wanted to go."

Ann has thrown herself into the work at Palacky University with the same intensity that has marked her teaching on three different continents for much of her life. In addition to supervising all second-year English teaching in the Philosophical Faculty, she does classroom teaching and instructs in special intensive English classes outside the university during semester breaks. Her teaching, in fact, never stops. She has but two modest rooms in the girls' dormitory for her living quarters, but during much of her "off-duty" time her sitting room is filled with students drinking tea and talking with the teacher.

Ann's explanation for giving so much of herself is uncomplicated. "To be effective," she says, "you have to care more about your students than yourself."

Will she retire again after finishing her Peace Corps assignment? Ann smiles at the question and answers, "I will go back to North Carolina and rest for a bit. Then I want to go to Hungary and use my brain a little by learning Hungarian. It's the most difficult language in Europe, you know."

"I Learn Something Every Day"

LIKE Ann Kurtz, Peace Corps volunteer Michael Schwartz lives and teaches in a Czech town of great age. Cheb, an ancient Bohemian town, is located less than five kilometers from the German border and until World War I was a part of Germany. There is a church near the main square that was built in the thirteenth century; Cheb Castle was built by Emperor Frederick Barbarossa in the twelfth century. Cheb is very close to three famous western Bohemian spa towns, which attracted notables such as Mark Twain from around the world in the last century.

Janet and Gary Gragg are also Peace Corps volunteers in Cheb. Married couples are welcome in the Peace Corps as long as both have the credentials for service. Janet was a registered nurse for twenty-five years in Madisonville, Kentucky; now she teaches conversational English to nurses at a Cheb hospital. Gary has a master's degree in English from the University of Kentucky and taught English for three years before switching to health administration. He was in charge of nine offices in the state health department in western Kentucky. In Cheb, Gary teaches English at the Economics Faculty of Western Bohemia.

Michael Schwartz with some of his students.

"When I tell my students about our old American cities, they just laugh at me," Michael says.

Michael is twenty-five, comes from Seattle, and earned a bachelor of arts degree in English from the University of Washington. He also has a degree in secondary education and middle school education. "The Peace Corps had been on my mind the entire time at the university," Michael says, "and I decided that before I settled down and got into a groove I would do this first. This has been a great learning experience. Eventually I want to teach geography and social studies and living here, meeting new people, taking part in another culture, has been invaluable. I learn something every day. I'm even thinking about staying an additional year. I love my students, and the other teachers have given me lots of support. They call me 'Maly'—that means Junior. We've become a family.''

Michael teaches a heavy schedule, twenty-eight hours a week, because there is a shortage of English teachers in his school. "I arrived in Cheb on a Thursday, visited the school on Friday, and started to teach on Monday," Michael says. "Five minutes before my first class was due to start, the students came and said they wanted to take me on a grand tour of Cheb. It was a good way to start our relationship. We have formed an English club, and even students who have graduated come back from the university and visit the club. One of my students, a graduate, told me how much he looked forward to club nights on Friday and the good conversation. Some of our sessions go on for as long as four hours.''

Michael is well into his second year in Cheb and is accumulating many good memories. He remembers one of them with particular warmth. "Last year the mother of one of my students made a special, traditional American Christmas dinner for me, with turkey and dressing, vegetables, everything. It was the first turkey she had ever cooked. Their Christmas is on the twenty-fourth, and she had cooked her family's traditional dinner the day before. This one was just for me, and of course I did it justice.''

5

The Peace Corps in Bulgaria

Peace Corps volunteers Frank Yanichek (standing, center) and Stephen King (standing, right) are small business volunteers in the Bulgarian city of Stara Zagora. They are involved in everything from helping start a peanut butter factory to assisting a local government-run radio and television station become privately owned. They are also helping a local trade school (shown here) whose students come from minority groups, broken homes, and orphanages.

IN THE early part of this century, Sofia, the capital city of Bulgaria, was known as the Paris of the Balkans, a pleasant, lively city of sidewalk cafes, art galleries, and vigorous intellectual activity. But after World War II, Bulgaria became such an obedient Communist satellite that it was often called the "sixteenth republic of the Soviet Union." Sofia, badly damaged in the war, became a cheerless city of ugly apartment blocks and dull government-owned stores. The spirited free press and book publishing companies were quickly a thing of the past and Sofia was no longer called the Paris of the Balkans except as a sarcastic joke. Communism quickly smothered the entire country. Private ownership became illegal, and all businesses and factories were absorbed by the government. Agricultural land was taken away from individual owners and became part of inefficient state-run collective farms.

But just as people in other Eastern European countries had been

Peace Corps volunteer Matt Brown, who teaches English at a Stara Zagora high school, is finding life in Bulgaria a thoroughly satisfying experience. "My closest Bulgarian friends are incredibly kind, considerate," he says. "There is a great sense of sharing with them. They ask wonderful questions about me and about America. I like the Bulgarian traditions, the things that are passed on from generation to generation: food, music, handicrafts, the clothes that are still worn from the old days."

biding their time, so had the Bulgarian people. On November 10, 1989, they ousted Todor Zhivkov, who had been Bulgaria's heavy-handed Communist boss for thirty-five years. A week later, fifty thousand people marched in Sofia demanding free elections and an end to police repression. Elections were held in June, and a non-Communist president was voted into office.

Sarah Heath, a businesswoman from California and former Peace Corps volunteer who served in Africa, is now director of the Peace Corps program in Bulgaria. Like many other outsiders, she watches the resurgence of the country with fascination and optimism. "The Bulgarians are a sophisticated people who have been under a heavy cloak for a long time," she says. "You might say that they have endured a long hard winter. Now things are changing and changing quickly. They're cleaning up Sofia, sweeping the streets. There is a tremendous surge of small business activity. New stores are opening up all around us."

Sarah's observations are on target. More than 200,000 persons have filed applications to go into business for themselves under the newly restored free-enterprise system. Eager entrepreneurs are not waiting until they have a store and plenty of capital. Two or three tables set up on a busy city street and loaded with previously banned books constitute a small business in Sofia today. Next to the books, another table piled high with blue jeans will be drawing a swarm of customers. In the rural areas collective farms are being closed down as quickly as possible and the land returned to the persons from whom it was taken over forty years ago.

Bulgaria has made a faster start in returning to a free-market system than most experts believed possible, but the forty years of Communist economic failure will be a hard hill to climb. The Western nations will have to help, and the Peace Corps' hand of friendship was one of the first to be extended.

"This Isn't Your Father's Peace Corps"

AS IN the other ex-Communist countries of Europe, the change to capitalism in Bulgaria is a task of monumental and bewildering proportions. Under communism almost everything was taken from the people and became government property, not only farms and factories but even food shops, clothing stores, and restaurants. Now this confiscated property must be given back. But how? And to whom? And over what length of time? After the toppling of communism, the Bulgarian parliament and president began immediately to guide the return to a private-enterprise system. This high-level process in still in progress.

It is at the municipal level—in the cities and towns of Bulgaria—that much of the actual work of changing government ownership to private ownership goes on. The business term for the changeover is "privatizing." Peace Corps volunteers in a number of Bulgarian cities are assisting municipal authorities in this difficult and often perplexing work.

Steve Butts is a small-business volunteer who works in Haskovo, a city of 100,000 about 130 miles south of Sofia and close to Bulgaria's border with Greece and Turkey. Steve is thirty-five and has a degree in accounting from the University of Dayton. He has worked as a certified public accountant in Cincinnati and in corporate accounting and finance in Florida. On the job in Haskovo he wears a jacket and tie, carries a briefcase, and very much projects the image of the successful young businessman he was in America.

Steve's work is divided roughly into two parts. The first involves helping the city government privatize the many small businesses that were handed to it (and to many other Bulgarian city governments) by the central government, to speed the work of private enterprise. Haskovo now finds itself the owner of roughly thirty restaurants and forty-five other businesses, including food shops, hotels, a bread factory, a clothing factory, and such miscellaneous shops as television repair, watch repair, and tombstone preparation! Under communism all of these businesses had been government-owned.

"We have drawn up a plan that will let local people buy these establishments over the next few years," Steve says. "The privatization process is complicated further by the fact that former owners, or their descendents, will be given back the businesses seized from them in the late forties. At home I did a lot of work on company mergers and acquisitions, and that has proven to be valuable experience for the work I am doing here."

Steve is a bit amused when he thinks about the work he is doing in the Peace Corps. "It isn't like digging wells in Africa, is it? The old Peace Corps didn't do the kind of work we're doing here in Bulgaria. In training we came up with a slogan—This Isn't Your Father's Peace Corps—and put it on T-shirts."

In fact, the Peace Corps is still digging wells in Africa, but Steve is right: much of its work in Eastern Europe is new territory for the Peace Corps.

"After privatization takes place," says Steve, "the other side of my job takes over. I have to work with these new business owners and help them make it in the world of private enterprise. Right now there is nothing printed in Bulgarian about what a small businessman needs to do in order to survive."

Steve's major success in Haskovo thus far is putting the clothing factory on a sound financial footing. "The former Communist managers of the factory layered so much debt on it that the interest came to $50,000 a month. I got the factory manager to negotiate with a local bank, and in exchange for a factory building—which the factory didn't need and which the bank will use for office

Steve Butts (center) at the Haskovo clothing factory.

space—the bank forgave a loan of a million dollars. Now without the debt the factory can be profitable to the tune of thirty to forty thousand dollars a month. The factory survives and two hundred to three hundred jobs a month are saved."

Sometimes when he has American visitors, Steve takes them for lunch at an outdoor cafe, one that has been privatized or soon will be. The Haskovans linger at the tables, enjoying the sunshine and an extra cup of coffee. "Their whole approach to life here is different," Steve tells his visitors. "They love to just sit and talk. They couldn't fathom how we live in America, that we shave in our cars, eat in our cars, dress in our cars."

Steve doesn't say it, but you believe he is thinking that Bulgarians have something to teach Americans, too.

"*Bez Dumi!* I'm Without Words!"

DAVID KINSLEY calls his players around him and says to them, "Grab a glove. Start throwing the ball around. But start slowly. Take care of your arm."

Thirty-five players, boys and girls in almost equal number, trot onto the field, and soon baseballs are whizzing around. The metallic sound of bat hitting ball mixes in with a lot of infield chatter. David watches the practice with the intensity of a coach getting ready for a big game.

"Two hands, Buddy!" he yells at an outfielder who tries a one-handed catch of an easy fly ball and drops it.

"Stretch when you make that catch and fire it home," he calls to a first baseman.

A second baseman throws to the wrong base, and David walks out to him. "Think what you're going to do before you get the ball," he tells the boy. "There's no time to think after you get it."

Except for the mixture of boys and girls, this might be baseball practice at almost any U.S. high school. But it isn't. David Kinsley is a Peace Corps volunteer who teaches English at a high school in Haskovo, the same Bulgarian city where his volunteer friend Steve Butts works. And the students so engrossed in practice had never seen a baseball or a bat until a few months ago.

"These kids love baseball," David says. "I'm amazed at how it has taken off. In class one day I explained a number of sports not played much in Bulgaria, if at all. I crumpled up a piece of paper and used a ruler as a bat. I even had one of the kids be a mock base runner. The students' imagination responded. They wanted to try baseball. It took some searching but I found a bat. For a while we had to use a tennis ball, but they weren't satisfied with that. I got the International Baseball Federation in Seattle to send us some equipment—baseballs, softballs, gloves—and I got stuff from home, but we still need catching equipment.

"Last year they were so enthusiastic we played right through the winter. They don't have a lot of things to do after school except for their books. I just wanted them to have fun and a lot of laughter. Baseball brings kids together from various schools. Now they've reached the point where they want to get serious. We've had one game with kids from another town, trained by another Peace Corps volunteer. There was a ton of spirit. By next spring we may have a real team."

David points to a girl in a purple jacket. "If we had baseball every day, she would be here. The girls are at least as enthusiastic as the boys." David points to the boy who is pitching. "He's one of the best. Last winter he asked me about his chances of playing professionally in the United States!"

David Kinsley (in white) watching batting practice with a critical eye.

David, who is twenty-six, grew up near Springfield, Massachusetts, and earned a bachelor of arts degree in English literature from Dartmouth College. Between graduation from college and joining the Peace Corps he lived on Nantucket Island and worked as a reporter for the *Nantucket Beacon*. About his reasons for becoming a Peace Corps volunteer, David says, "I wanted to shake things up in my life. It had become too comfortable, too easy. When I heard about the new Peace Corps program in Europe, it struck a chord in me. I believe in service."

75

Peace Corps volunteer Don Baggo teaches English at a school in Vraca, a small Bulgarian city north of Sofia. Don is presently savoring a successful student production at school of the play Our Town by American author Thornton Wilder. "Why did we choose this play by Wilder?" Don says, repeating a question. "A small town in Bulgaria is not that much different from one in the United States. Daily life is the same. You get up in the morning, have a cup of coffee, go to work, fall in love, get married, die. There is a universal message in the play." Before joining the Peace Corps Don taught English in several Minnesota high schools and was principal of the Huntly, Minnesota, high school.

David takes his teaching very seriously. "The drive of these kids is incredible," he says. "English is seen as a ticket to the future, a means of opening doors to jobs. But it's more than that. Knowing English opens up our literature, films, magazines. It opens up our whole culture.

"But," David continues, "in a sense, I teach a course in life. We talk about politics, books, sports, all kinds of things. There's a tremendous curiosity about America and anything related to it."

David's energy seems unlimited. In addition to his regular English teaching and baseball, he teaches a course after school in preparing to take the Scholastic Aptitude Test (S.A.T.), which most foreign students applying for entrance to U.S. colleges and universities must take (together with a test of their English-language proficiency). Attending David's S.A.T. course is voluntary and is made up of the top students in the school, all of whom have hopes of going to college in America.

The intense interest of his students gave David still another idea. "My kids had a dream of going to the United States and, simply put, I wanted to make the dream come true, for some of them, at least. So I planned a trip home."

The big problem, of course, was money. David began by soliciting funds from U.S. foundations; but he knew that to get help from them, he would have to show Bulgarian support for the idea. To get local support, David organized a Haskovo Marathon—before Peace Corps he had run in the Boston Marathon—and tied it in with the U.S. trip for the sake of publicity. Haskovo merchants who contributed to the trip got publicity in the marathon. Eventually they raised $20,000 from all sources, enough to take twelve students, two adult Bulgarian chaperones, and David to the United States. David's top students were chosen for the trip.

"I wanted to make it more than a sightseeing trip," David says, recalling the memorable two weeks, "so we made it a service-oriented project to explore the role and responsibility of a student in a democracy. How do you build a community and how do you make it work? We met with the mayor of Springfield, journalists, teachers. In collaboration with local high school students, we served meals to the homeless in Springfield—they needed to know that the United States has its problems, too. They joined with Springfield students in planting flowers as part of a civic beautification project. On Nantucket my kids taught ten-year-olds about Bulgaria. Of course, we had fun, too. We had top seats for a Red Sox ball game, for example. The trip worked on so many different levels. It was magical. The kids were overwhelmed. They kept saying, '*Bez dumi!* I'm without words!' They were impressed by the kindness of Americans. And by American smiles. Here in Bulgaria people don't smile as much, because of their problems.''

IN Steve Butts and David Kinsley the city of Haskovo has two quite different kinds of Peace Corps volunteers. A bit older, with years of experience in small business development, Steve is typical of the new, more professional Peace Corps. With his energy, his enthusiasm, his imagination, David is an example of the young volunteers who have been making a difference in the Peace Corps for more than thirty years.

In one way, the most important way of all, Steve and David are the same: the desire to be of service. Haskovo is fortunate to have them both.

6

The Peace Corps
in Romania

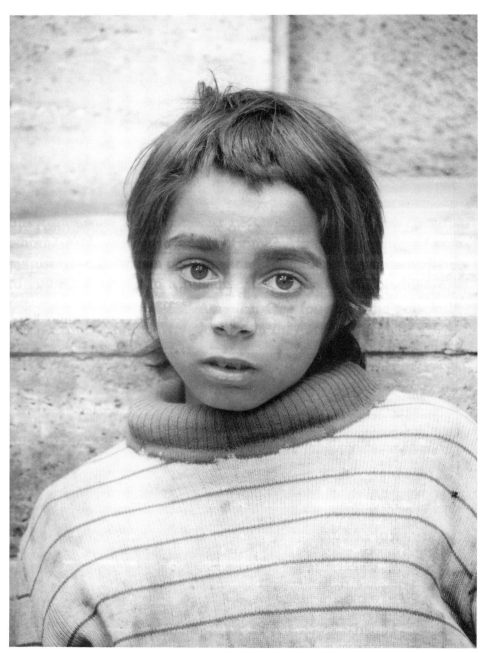

A street child in Bucharest.

COMMUNIST rule in Romania was harsher than in any other Eastern European satellite country. With the help of Russian advisers, the Romanian army became a government tool for social and political control; a secret police force called the Securitate was created and spread fear and uncertainty throughout the land. During the regime of absolute dictator Nicolae Ceausescu (1965–1989) political repression grew to suffocating proportions. All independent social organizations were destroyed or absorbed by the Communist government; all individually owned farms were pulled into "collectivized" agriculture.

The throwing off of Communist rule was accomplished without violence in Poland, Czechoslovakia, Hungary, and Bulgaria. Part of the reason was that Communist government leaders in those countries had permitted some limited free expression and the development of some civil organizations such as Solidarity in Poland. There was no such relaxation of rigid control in Romania, but even Ceausescu's iron hand could not prevent the revolt of the people that swept Eastern Europe in 1989. And in Romania the revolution was not peaceful but violent and bloody.

Jacqueline Stark is an energetic sixty-four-year-old Peace Corps volunteer teacher in the Romanian city of Sibiu. She is so well adjusted and enjoys her work so much that she is thinking about staying in Romania after her Peace Corps service. "I can teach or tutor," she says. "I like working. So did my mother. I must have a work gene. I tried retirement once and hated it." Jackie (as everyone calls her) teaches English to ninth and tenth graders.

Ann Hartman teaches English at a high school in Stara Zagora. "I see myself as a bearer of fresh ideas," she says. "These kids have been shut off. They have no notion of what else is out there in the world."

Antigovernment demonstrations began in the Transylvanian city of Timisoara on December 16 and quickly spread to Bucharest, the capital. The army and the secret police were called out, and the secret police began to fire into the crowds. But the demonstrators appealed to the army troops to join them in the protests, and the army responded, firing back at the police. Over a thousand people were killed in the fighting, but in time government forces began to crumble. Nicolae Ceausescu and his wife tried to flee the country, but they were caught, quickly tried by a military court, and executed. Thus did another Eastern European Communist regime come to an end.

This homeless street boy is better off than most because he has been given warm clothes and a good pair of shoes.

Because of the extreme repression of the Ceausescu years, Romania may have a longer road to travel to find its way to a workable democratic capitalism. But a start has been made. The Romanian people have approved a new constitution; two rounds of local, parliamentary, and presidential elections have been held since the overthrow of the Communist government.

A Peace Corps staff member in Bucharest made this interesting observation: "In parts of Eastern Europe, during the dark years, cultural life suffered, but here in Romania it continued to flourish and no doubt helped the Romanian people to survive. One evening I walked from the office to my apartment. It was warm and apartment windows along the way were open. There was a symphony being performed on the radio and from almost every open window I passed, I could hear the music, follow it along as I got closer to home. That experience symbolized Romania to me."

The Invisible Children

BUCHAREST is full of homeless children, as many as four thousand according to one study. Thousands more prowl the streets of other Romanian cities. But unless you are looking for them, unless you know they are there, they are almost invisible. You see them darting out in the middle of traffic to clean windshields at stoplights. On a street corner they tug at a passerby's sleeve and beg for money, then disappear in case a policeman is watching. They sleep in doorways and dig for food in alley garbage bins. But always they try to stay out of sight because the police are their enemies.

These hopeless children are a legacy of the dictator Nicolae

Ceausescu who stifled all Romanian programs of charity, social services, and family planning. To allow such programs would have been an admission that there were economic and social problems in Romania. The official government line was that there were no such problems. Hence there was no need for welfare departments and social workers. Over time these departments and schools for training social workers were shut down. But in the bleak economic conditions of Romania, parents abandoned their children or the children ran away from intolerable conditions at home. In addition to the street children, as many as 200,000 other children were "warehoused" in run-down state institutions and orphanages when the people revolted against dictator Nicolae Ceausescu. Medical services were appalling and educational facilities almost nonexistent. These forlorn young Romanians have become known as "Ceausescu's children."

Although major upgrading will take years, a start has been made by the new post-Communist Romanian government in improving conditions in state-run institutions for unwanted children. Improving the lot of street children has been even slower and has been left largely to private charitable and church-based organizations. The shelter where Peace Corps volunteer Tom Ritter works is funded by Caritas, a Catholic charity headquartered in Germany.

In addition to working in the shelter, Tom spends a part of every day at the Gara du Nord, Bucharest's main train station, where many street children spend a large part of their days and nights. The Gara is a huge, dark, dispiriting place, but during the day it is jammed with commuters from whom the kids can beg. It is filled with shabby kiosks and cafes from which they can beg a handout or—at some risk—pilfer something to eat. At night they can sleep in dark corners or sometimes in an idled railroad car.

Tom leaves the shelter every afternoon with a big red plastic bag filled with sandwiches. He takes a bus to the train station and

Tom Ritter with one of the younger boys at the shelter for homeless children.

immediately upon entering the cavernous building is swarmed over by kids with outstretched hands. For most of them the sandwich Tom gives them will be their only food for the day. But no matter how many sandwiches he stuffs into the bag, there are never enough. Always some of the children walk away empty-handed.

Afterward Tom walks around the station looking for children. There is little he can do but talk with them, show his concern, and sometimes—if there seems to be a pressing medical problem—try to find help. On this day Paul is with Tom, and they encounter two children wandering in the dark, gloomy depths of the station. Tom estimates that they are four or five years old. He talks to them. They do not know if they have any family. They do not know how long they have been living on the streets.

Paul says, "No matter how precocious a child is, he isn't able to take care of himself at four or five. Where will they sleep tonight?"

"Here," Tom says, "at the Gara."

"What about the police?" Paul asks. "Can't they do something?"

"The police focus is to get rid of the kids," Tom says. "Every one of these kids has a police story to tell."

A few minutes later they meet a fifteen-year-old gypsy girl, one of the lucky ones who got a sandwich that day. She reports that the police had conducted a one A.M. roundup the night before. After beating the kids, the police carted them off to a distant lockup. The girl continues to talk in Romanian to Tom, and after she leaves, he tells Paul, "She said the police ordered her to put her hands on a rail and then started beating them with a stick."

Tom is silent a moment then continues, "One day a Romanian shelter staffer and I were taking sandwiches to the Gara when we came on a policeman violently kicking a little boy on the ground. When we asked him to stop, he started hitting us with his stick. I saw some horrible things happening to the homeless in Chicago, but it was just now and then. Here it is every day and it's directed at children.''

Back at the shelter Tom pitches in to help get ready for the nightly invasion of street children and for their dinner. But he is troubled by the memory of the two four-year-olds that he and Paul saw at the Gara du Nord that afternoon. "I've got to find some way to start an outreach program," he says. "There has to be some way to help kids like that."

"We Want to Change the System"

PEACE CORPS volunteer Mary Yendrick lives and works in Brasov, one of Romania's major cities. Brasov lies three hours by train north of Bucharest, and there is a timeless quality about the Romanian countryside between these two cities. Fields are plowed by oxen; crops are harvested by hand. Big flocks of sheep graze in fields with their shepherds standing like statues. But the modern world intrudes in places. The train goes through Ploesti, with its big oil refinery. During World War II Ploesti was the target of many Allied bomber planes.

Mary lives in an apartment provided by the city. From her balcony all you can see is an endless line of apartment blocks, all exactly like the building she lives in. Other Romanian cities are jammed with the same faceless apartment buildings, a legacy of Communist development. "I call it Blockland," says Mary, "because everyone lives in them."

Brasov lies in a scenic stretch of the Carpathian Mountains. A luxurious ski resort is located just above the city, but it might as well be on another planet for all the use the residents of Blockland get out of it.

Mary is twenty-seven and, like Tom Ritter in Bucharest, she calls Chicago home. She earned a bachelor's degree in political science at Eastern Illinois University and a master's degree in educational psychology from the same school. She worked as an abuse and neglect caseworker with children in foster care institutions for two-and-a-half years in Champaign and Chicago.

"That was good training for Romania," Mary says.

Mary is one of the first generation of Peace Corps volunteers in Romania, one of eighteen who arrived in early 1991 to work in orphanages. They were split into teams of three and sent to Moldavia, the poorest part of the country, where Mary wound up working at an orphanage in Piatra Meamt. From the beginning the assignments were fuzzy, not well thought out. Most of the volunteers resigned in frustration, but Mary was one of the few who refused to quit.

"The orphanages didn't have a real role for us," she recalls, "so we just sat there. I'd go there every day, but nobody cared what I did. I was on my own. I'm the type of person who works best with goals and support. I was the token foreigner. They'd trot me out whenever we had visitors at the orphanage. Eventually I found a ward of AIDS babies that nobody was interested in. I did what I could working by myself; but after nine months I was transferred here to Brasov, where I started working with a shelter for homeless children."

The shelter was a small place, just two rooms, one for staff, a larger one for twenty children—the same type of street children who come to Tom Ritter's shelter in Bucharest. "Mostly there were boys with very aggressive, violent tendencies," Mary says. "A boy had his eye poked out the first week I was there.

Mary Yendrick and Damien.

"They were locked in one room with nothing to do, no school, no games, no structure. It was like a pressure cooker. I knew I had found my place! I worked there for three months. I would play with the kids, give them things to do. I found crayons and let them color. They would go crazy with just a little stimulation. They had never had any attention like that in their entire lives."

The homeless shelter was only an interim assignment, and after three months Mary joined the staff of the Romanian Orphanage

Trust. "It's a wonderful British organization," Mary explains, "and we're working with the Ministry of Labor and Social Protection to find foster care families for children in orphanages."

This is a pilot effort to introduce a foster care program, the first of its kind in Romania. The pilot program is being tested in four counties; if it works, it will become a national system.

Mary is part of a team: a newly trained Romanian social worker, an Irish social worker, and herself. They spend their days interviewing families who are interested in having foster children. "We want to prove that foster care works," Mary says. "We want to show that it can be much better for the children and much less expensive than to keep them in institutions. We want to change the system."

Part of Mary's work is to visit a pediatric hospital and check on abandoned children who have been brought there by police. At the hospital, she introduces a Peace Corps visitor to a bright-eyed little boy, who came in sick after his parents abandoned him fifteen months ago. "The staff has given him the name Damien," Mary tells her visitor. "He's a good prospect for foster care or even adoption because he's so intelligent and verbal." And she adds, "When we can, we like to get the children before they get into the orphanage system."

That night as Mary and her visitor are walking through the darkened streets to a restaurant, they encounter a young boy walking along with a satchel in his hand. Mary and the boy are happy to see each other because he had been one of her shelter children. She kisses him on the cheek, and he tells her that he is living with a woman now and going to school. Mary remembers when he arrived at the shelter, after police had picked him up at the train station. His head had been shaved and was covered with bumps where he had been beaten.

After Mary and the boy part, she says to her visitor, "It makes me a little anxious, his walking here so late at night." Mary's case-worker experience never lets her relax. "I will check on him to-morrow to make sure that everything is all right."

"We've Been Waiting a Long Time for You"

PEACE CORPS volunteers Derica Griffiths and Julie Hillebrand are having experiences in Romania quite different from those of Tom Ritter and Mary Yendrick. Derica and Julie teach English in two good Bucharest high schools; their students come from homes where they have received the love and attention that the children Tom and Mary work with have never known.

"Teaching these kids is so easy," Julie says. "Of course, they are not accustomed to the way I teach. They are not used to having their teachers ask their opinions. I talk to them one-on-one and get down to their level. They ask me questions all the time about the United States, and that has made me think about and focus on my own country. Being here has made me much more aware of myself as an American."

Derica teaches at a high school with a business-commercial ori-entation. "It's good for the students to hear how a native speaker uses English," she says, "but it's not enough for me to come here and teach them how to speak the language properly. These students don't understand democracy, what being free means. They don't understand what it is to express themselves freely in a classroom. I spend the first fifteen minutes of every hour just talking to them. It is not something they are accustomed to. When I first came, they didn't trust me; they didn't believe the Peace Corps volunteers would

Julie Hillebrand's students gather around her after class for some fun talk.

stay. They were very quiet and reserved. Under the old regime there were subjects they couldn't even consider. We have to show them that they can take control of their destiny, change their country."

Derica explains her being in Romania this way. "Peace Corps commercials on television planted the seeds of doing something like this in my head when I was very young. I wanted to touch the world and be touched. It was my dream. At first I was afraid because I had student loans to pay off. As corny as it sounds, we all have to believe that we can make the world a better place."

Julie Hillebrand and Derica Griffiths shopping in a Bucharest market. As everywhere in this part of Europe, there has been an explosion of entrepreneurship, of people setting up a table and selling all sorts of items. With winter approaching, Julie and Derica were looking for heavy coats. There were some, but they were all too expensive for their limited Peace Corps living allowance.

Julie and Derica each has a spartanly furnished room in a hundred-year-old building attached to Derica's school. Water is erratic, sometimes only once a week; and if they are lucky, heat will be turned on at the end of November. Other problems of living in Bucharest are the scarcity of fruits and vegetables sometimes and their limited Peace Corps living allowance which, in the inflated market, puts some food and clothes out of their reach. Still, they sometimes feel guilty that they are not living the more rugged type of Peace Corps existence that some volunteers in Africa, Asia, and Latin America live.

Julie says, "People at home ask me about hardships, and I tell them I went to the opera last night!"

Still, it is not like living at home. "On weekends when we visit our friends it is a treat to take a bath in hot water," Derica says.

Both Derica and Julie have made good friends in Romania. "These people are so nice and so hospitable that it has been easy to become part of their culture," Julie explains. "The Romanian woman I stayed with during training has become my best friend."

Derica agrees. "They have welcomed us with open arms. One woman said to me, "We have been waiting a long time for you."

7

The Next Peace Corps Frontier

Mary Yendrick in a pediatric hospital in Romania, with a child who was abandoned by his parents.

THE Peace Corps sent volunteers into the new frontier of Eastern Europe in 1990. Since that beginning of 121 volunteers in Hungary and Poland, the number has grown to over 500 in 1993, and the countries of Bulgaria, the Czech Republic, Slovakia, Romania, and Albania have been added.

But even as the Peace Corps was establishing programs in Eastern Europe, another frontier appeared on the horizon, even farther to the east. In 1991 the Soviet Union itself, the giant Communist empire that covered over eight-and-a-half million square miles of Europe and Asia, came apart. Each of the fifteen "republics" that made up the Soviet Union declared its independence, and together they formed the Commonwealth of Independent States.

Hardly had the vibrations ceased from the dramatic political explosion than most of the newly independent countries began to express interest in receiving Peace Corps volunteers. Country agreements were quickly drawn up, and by early 1993 about 300 volunteers were at work in Russia, Ukraine, Armenia, Uzbekistan, and the Baltic countries of Estonia, Latvia, and Lithuania. By the end of 1993 volunteers will go to four other former Soviet Union countries: Kazakhstan, Kirghistan, Turkmenistan, and Moldova. The work of most volunteers in these countries is to assist in the transition from a government-controlled economy to a free-enterprise system. Five hundred volunteers are expected to be at work by 1994, and the number may go much higher after that.

The volunteers in Russia and elsewhere in the former Soviet Union are being overwhelmed with kindness and genuine affection. The very thought that it is no longer dangerous to have a foreigner, especially an American, in one's home is a wondrous thing. The situation in Russia and the rest of the region is still highly unstable, and no one knows with any certainty what the future will bring. One thing is certain, however: the Peace Corps is building bridges of understanding where previously there were none.

ANOTHER frontier of the Peace Corps has always been the United States itself. The first two objectives of the Peace Corps are to help other countries meet their needs for trained workers and to further a better understanding of the American people on the part of the people served. The Peace Corps' third objective is to increase America's understanding of other peoples and cultures.

For most volunteers the accomplishment of the third objective has been almost automatic. Many are the volunteers who have said, "We learned more than we taught." And many are the volunteers who have made teaching their careers after returning from Peace Corps service, bringing their special knowledge of other countries into the classroom. Many more have used their experience in other kinds of public service.

"Come back and educate us," President Kennedy said to the first volunteers who went overseas in 1961.

Since that time over 130,000 volunteers have served in more than one hundred countries around the world. Most, upon returning to the United States, have tried to do what the man who created the Peace Corps asked them to do.

Index